Honoring Our
Veterans

LEISURE ARTS, INC. • Maumelle, Arkansas

EDITORIAL STAFF

Vice President of Editorial: Susan White Sullivan
Creative Art Director: Katherine Laughlin
Publications Director: Leah Lampirez
Special Projects Director: Susan Frantz Wiles
Technical Writer: Lois J. Long
Technical Editors: Linda A. Daley, Sarah J. Green,
    and Cathy Hardy
Art Category Manager: Lora Puls
Graphic Artist: Jacqueline Breazeal
Prepress Technician: Stephanie Johnson
Contributing Photographer: Ken West
Contributing Photo Stylist: Sondra Daniel

BUSINESS STAFF

President and Chief Executive Officer:
    Fred F. Pruss
Senior Vice President of Operations:
    Jim Dittrich
Vice President of Retail Sales:
    Martha Adams
Vice President of Mass Market Sales:
    Bob Bewighouse
Vice President of Technology and Planning:
    Laticia Mull Dittrich
Controller: Tiffany P. Childers
Information Technology Director: Brian Roden
Director of E-Commerce: Mark Hawkins
Manager of E-Commerce: Robert Young

Afghans made and instructions tested by Janet Akins, JoAnn
Bowling, Marianna Crowder, Raymelle Greening, Dale Potter,
and Margaret Taverner.

ISBN-13/EAN: 978-1-4647-0937-1

INTRODUCTION

Show your gratitude to veterans and active members of the Armed Forces and their families with comforting throws and lap robes. These 13 designs are all crocheted with American-made yarn in patriotic colors or camouflage prints.

26

BONUS

LOOK FOR THE CAMERA
in our instructions and watch our bonus technique videos made just for you!
www.LeisureArts.com/6081

TABLE OF CONTENTS

6

13

22

Meet the Designer: Carolyn Pfeifer

Believing that most people have been touched in some way by a veteran or active service member, Carolyn Pfeifer wanted to design easy throws that even beginners could make for family or charitable giving. "My Dad was a World War II veteran and spoke of his experiences and his buddies all the time," she said. Inspired by the variety of camo yarns available, "it was clear to me that it was something I wanted to do to honor them as well as all veterans." Carolyn finds time for crochet around her work as a full-time hairstylist.

VETERAN SALUTE

This is a small, small world, especially when it comes to the connections between American citizens and the veterans who have served in various branches of the United States military. It seems every American family has direct ties to veterans and active service members, whether they are immediate family, extended family, neighbors, co-workers, the mail carrier, the local mechanic, or part of some other group.

Honor, courage, and commitment have defined the lives of these men and women, and they will forever deserve our respect and gratitude. And we also must acknowledge the sacrifices that their families have made for us. How can we ever repay them? Any show of respect goe a long way. Crocheters as a group are known for the generous hearts and for their conviction that a warr handmade throw is the equivalent of caring hug.

All of the designs in this book are crochete with American-made yarn in patrioti colors or camouflage prints — perfect fo a veteran or family member. There is eve one inspired by the American flag. Twelv of the 13 designs are each sized for both lap robe and a throw.

Start one today for a veteran you know, or check ou the tips on the next page to reach out to deservin veterans everywhere.

MADE IN AMERICA, FOR AMERICANS

The *Super Saver®* and *With Love®* yarns used in this book are made in America by *Red Heart®*. For over 75 years, more people have chosen to make family heirlooms using Red Heart yarn than any other yarn. *Super Saver®* and *With Love®* are among 20 yarns that Red Heart proudly manufactures at its mill in Albany, Georgia.

MADE IN USA

The colors used in the photography models of each design are listed on page 48. However, you should feel free to choose other colors, especially if a different camo yarn would better represent your honoree's branch of service or experience. While some camo yarns closely resemble the jungle or desert colors familiar to many soldiers, others are great choices for family members who love camouflage patterns but don't have to worry about concealment for their survival.

We think Pink Camo (see page 39) is perfect for a female veteran or even a little girl whose father or mother (or favorite uncle or aunt) is away on active duty. Our photo on page 23 shows how Earth & Sky looks great in a room full of maps, such as you might find in the home of someone who served or grew up on bases around the world.

OMMUNITY OUTREACH

irst of all, simply look around ou to find veterans who might eed your gifts of comfort. Once ou've made throws or lap robes r those in your family or circle f friends, you can extend your elp to other veterans through ocal facilities. These include ospitals and clinics, veterans' rganizations, retirement homes, ursing homes, shelters, churches, ivic groups, and community ervice agencies. Many will ave active volunteer programs r auxiliary groups that you an contact about donating andmade items; some work year- ound but others gear up during olidays and other special times.

SPECIAL THANKS

e owe a special thanks to Leisure rts employees who shared their mily memorabilia for use in our hotography: Jean Lewis, Jim Dittrich, lark Hawkins, Martha Darbonne, arah Green, and Susan Wiles.

NATIONAL PROGRAMS

To reach beyond your hometown, consider sending your throws to an organization that responds to needs across the country or around the world. Ask for recommendations from your friends who knit or crochet, check online forums in social media groups or on knit and crochet industry websites, or go online and search, using keywords such as "charity crochet for veterans." Contact the groups directly, or consider organizations such as the ones listed here.

SOLDIERS' ANGELS

Soldiers' Angels is a volunteer-led, 501(c)(3) non-profit organization providing aid and comfort to the men and women of the United States Army, Marines, Navy, Air Force, Coast Guard, and their families. Hundreds of thousands of Angel volunteers assist veterans of all generations, wounded and deployed personnel and their families in a variety of unique and effective ways.

One way is through the Blankets of Gratitude program operated by the Soldiers' Angels Sewing Team sub-group, VA Crochet and Craft Team, whose mission is "making sure America's veterans know we still love and appreciate them." The team collects knitted, crocheted, and loomed blankets to give to hospitalized veterans. To learn more about how Soldiers' Angels supports veterans or troops and their families, visit **www.soldiersangels.org** and click on the site menu or the link under "Teams and Projects - How to Help" on the homepage.

WARM UP AMERICA!

Warm Up America! collects knitted and crocheted afghan blankets, clothing and accessories to bring comfort to people (including veterans) who have lost their homes, fled abusive relationships, or who are being cared for in hospices, shelters, hospitals, and nursing homes. Many thousands of handmade items are distributed to various charities each year.

Warm Up America! began in 1991 as a national grassroots program founded by Evie Rosen, encouraging knitters and crocheters to use their scrap yarn to make 7" by 9" blocks that could be combined into afghans for the needy. With the help of the Craft Yarn Council, a non-profit association of yarn companies and publishers, Warm Up America! became a 501(c)(3) tax exempt, charitable organization. Through the years it has provided more than 250,000 afghans for people in need.

Because of the large volume of blocks it receives, the organization encourages you to work locally whenever possible to complete and donate your afghans. For free block patterns and more information, visit the Foundation's website at **www.WarmUpAmerica.org** or write to Warm Up America! Foundation, 469 Hospital Drive, 2nd Floor Suite E, Gastonia, NC 28054.

AMERICAN HERO

 EASY

SHOPPING LIST

Yarn (Medium Weight) [MEDIUM 4]

[7 ounces, 364 yards
(198 grams, 333 meters) per skein]:

☐ Red - 2{3} skeins

☐ Tan - 2{3} skeins

☐ Blue - 2{3} skeins

When purchasing yarn, reference
the Blue number for skeins needed
for the Lap Robe and the Pink
number for skeins needed for the
Afghan.

Crochet Hook

☐ Size I (5.5 mm)
or size needed for gauge

Additional Supplies

☐ Yarn needle

Our photography
model was made using
Red Heart® Super Saver®

MADE IN USA

SIZE INFORMATION

Finished Sizes
Lab Robe: 39½" x 49" (100.5 cm x 124.5 cm)
Afghan: 49" x 58½" (124.5 cm x 148.5 cm)

Size Note: We have printed the instructions for the sizes in
different colors to make it easier for you to find:

• Lap Robe in Blue

• Afghan in Pink

Instructions in Black apply to both sizes.

GAUGE INFORMATION

Gauge Swatch: 4¾" (12 cm) square
Work same as Square A, page 8: 48 dc and 16 sps.

INSTRUCTIONS

Square A [Make 12{16}]

With Red, ch 4; join with slip st to form a ring.

Rnd 1 (Right side): Ch 3 (**counts as first dc, now and throughout**), 2 dc in ring, ch 2, (3 dc in ring, ch 2) 3 times; join with slip st to first dc: 12 dc and 4 ch-2 sps.

Note: Loop a short piece of yarn around any stitch to mark Rnd 1 as **right** side.

Rnd 2: Slip st in next 2 dc and in next ch-2 sp, ch 3, (2 dc, ch 2, 3 dc) in same sp, ch 1, ★ (3 dc, ch 2, 3 dc) in next ch-2 sp, ch 1; repeat from ★ 2 times **more**; join with slip st to first dc: 24 dc and 8 sps.

Rnd 3: Slip st in next 2 dc and in next ch-2 sp, ch 3, (2 dc, ch 2, 3 dc) in same sp, ch 1, 3 dc in next ch-1 sp, ch 1, ★ (3 dc, ch 2, 3 dc) in next ch-2 sp, ch 1, 3 dc in next ch-1 sp, ch 1; repeat from ★ 2 times **more**; join with slip st to first dc: 36 dc and 12 sps.

Rnd 4: Slip st in next 2 dc and in next ch-2 sp, ch 3, (2 dc, ch 2, 3 dc) in same sp, ch 1, (3 dc in next ch-1 sp, ch 1) twice, ★ (3 dc, ch 2, 3 dc) in next ch-2 sp, ch 1, (3 dc in next ch-1 sp, ch 1) twice; repeat from ★ 2 times **more**; join with slip st to first dc, finish off: 48 dc and 16 sps.

Square B [Make 12{16}]

With Tan, work same as Square A: 48 dc and 16 sps.

Square C [Make 12{16}]

With Red, ch 4; join with slip st to form a ring.

Rnd 1 (Right side): Ch 3, 2 dc in ring, ch 2, (3 dc in ring, ch 2) 3 times; join with slip st to first dc: 12 dc and 4 ch-2 sps.

Note: Mark Rnd 1 as **right** side.

Rnd 2: Slip st in next 2 dc and in next ch-2 sp, ch 3, (2 dc, ch 2, 3 dc) in same sp, ch 1, ★ (3 dc, ch 2, 3 dc) in next ch-2 sp, ch 1; repeat from ★ 2 times **more**; join with slip st to first dc, finish off: 24 dc and 8 sps.

Rnd 3: With **right** side facing, join Tan with slip st in any corner ch-2 sp, ch 3, (2 dc, ch 2, 3 dc) in same sp, ch 1, 3 dc in next ch-1 sp, ch 1, ★ (3 dc, ch 2, 3 dc) in next ch-2 sp, ch 1, 3 dc in next ch-1 sp, ch 1; repeat from ★ 2 times **more**; join with slip st to first dc: 36 dc and 12 sps.

Rnd 4: Slip st in next 2 dc and in next ch-2 sp, ch 3, (2 dc, ch 2, 3 dc) in same sp, ch 1, (3 dc in next ch-1 sp, ch 1) twice, ★ (3 dc, ch 2, 3 dc) in next ch-2 sp, ch 1, (3 dc in next ch-1 sp, ch 1) twice; repeat from ★ 2 times **more**; join with slip st to first dc, finish off: 48 dc and 16 sps.

Square D [Make 12{32}]

Work same as Square C working Rnds 1 and 2 with Tan and Rnds 3 and 4 with Red: 48 dc and 16 sps.

Square E [Make 28{36}]

Work same as Square C working Rnds 1 and 2 with Tan and Rnds 3 and 4 with Blue: 48 dc and 16 sps.

Square F (Make 4)

With Blue, ch 4; join with slip st to form a ring.

Rnd 1 (Right side)**:** Ch 3, 2 dc in ring, ch 2, (3 dc in ring, ch 2) 3 times; join with slip st to first dc, finish off: 12 dc and 4 ch-2 sps.

Note: Mark Rnd 1 as **right** side.

Rnd 2: With **right** side facing, join Tan with slip st in any ch-2 sp; ch 3, (2 dc, ch 2, 3 dc) in same sp, ch 1, ★ (3 dc, ch 2, 3 dc) in next ch-2 sp, ch 1; repeat from ★ 2 times **more**; join with slip st to first dc, finish off: 24 dc and 8 sps.

Rnd 3: With **right** side facing, join Blue with slip st in any corner ch-2 sp; ch 3, (2 dc, ch 2, 3 dc) in same sp, ch 1, 3 dc in next ch-1 sp, ch 1, ★ (3 dc, ch 2, 3 dc) in next ch-2 sp, ch 1, 3 dc in next ch-1 sp, ch 1; repeat from ★ 2 times **more**; join with slip st to first dc: 36 dc and 12 sps.

Rnd 4: Slip st in next 2 dc and in next ch-2 sp, ch 3, (2 dc, ch 2, 3 dc) in same sp, ch 1, (3 dc in next ch-1 sp, ch 1) twice, ★ (3 dc, ch 2, 3 dc) in next ch-2 sp, ch 1, (3 dc in next ch-1 sp, ch 1) twice; repeat from ★ 2 times **more**; join with slip st to first dc, finish off: 48 dc and 16 sps.

Assembly

With **wrong** sides together and corresponding color, using Placement Diagram as a guide and working through **both** loops on **both** pieces, 🎥 whipstitch *(Fig. 6, page 47)* Squares together, forming 8{10} vertical strips of 10{12} squares each, beginning in second ch of first corner ch-2 and ending in first ch of second corner ch-2; then whipstitch strips together in same manner.

Edging

Rnd 1: With **right** side facing, 🎥 join Blue with sc *(see Joining with Sc, page 46)* in any corner ch-2 sp; 2 sc in same sp, sc in next 3 dc, (sc in next ch-1 sp and in next 3 dc) 3 times,

★ † sc in next 2 sps and in next 3 dc, (sc in next ch-1 sp and in next 3 dc) 3 times †; repeat from † to † across to next corner ch-2 sp, 3 sc in corner sp, sc in next 3 dc, (sc in next ch-1 sp and in next 3 dc) 3 times; repeat from ★ 2 times **more**, then repeat from † to † across; join with slip st to first sc: 616{752} sc.

Rnd 2: Slip st in next sc, ch 3, 2 dc in same st, ★ dc in next sc and in each sc across to center sc of next corner 3-sc group, 3 dc in center sc; repeat from ★ 2 times **more**, dc in next sc and in each sc across; join with slip st to first dc, finish off.

AFGHAN
PLACEMENT DIAGRAM

F	E	E	E	E	E	E	E	E	F
E	A	A	A	A	A	A	A	A	E
E	D	D	D	D	D	D	D	D	E
E	B	B	B	B	B	B	B	B	E
E	C	C	C	C	C	C	C	C	E
E	D	D	D	D	D	D	D-	D	E
E	D	D	D	D	D	D	D	D	E
E	C	C	C	C	C	C	C	C	E
E	B	B	B	B	B	B	B	B	E
E	D	D	D	D	D	D	D	D	E
E	A	A	A	A	A	A	A	A	E
F	E	E	E	E	E	E	E	E	F

LAP ROBE
PLACEMENT DIAGRAM

F	E	E	E	E	E	E	F
E	A	A	A	A	A	A	E
E	D	D	D	D	D	D	E
E	B	B	B	B	B	B	E
E	C	C	C	C	C	C	E
E	C	C	C	C	C	C	E
E	B	B	B	B	B	B	E
E	D	D	D	D	D	D	E
E	A	A	A	A	A	A	E
F	E	E	E	E	E	E	F

AMERICAN INSPIRATION

 EASY

SHOPPING LIST

Yarn (Medium Weight) 〔MEDIUM 4〕

**[7 ounces, 370 yards
(198 grams, 338 meters) per skein]:**

☐ Red - 3{5} skeins

☐ Blue - 1{2} skein(s)

When purchasing yarn, reference the Blue number for skeins needed for the Lap Robe and the Pink number for skeins needed for the Afghan.

Crochet Hook

☐ Size I (5.5 mm)

or size needed for gauge

SIZE INFORMATION

Finished Sizes

Lab Robe: 36" x 47½" (91.5 cm x 120.5 cm)

Afghan: 47" x 60" (119.5 cm x 152.5 cm)

Size Note: We have printed the instructions for the sizes in different colors to make it easier for you to find:

• Lap Robe in Blue

• Afghan in Pink

Instructions in Black apply to both sizes.

GAUGE INFORMATION

In pattern, 18 sts = 5½" (14 cm);
    one repeat (Rows 4-11) = 4½" (11.5 cm)

Gauge Swatch: 5"w x 4½"h (12.75 cm x 11.5 cm)

With Red, ch 17.

Work same as Instructions, page 12, for 8 rows: 16 sts.

Finish off.

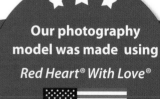

Our photography model was made using *Red Heart® With Love®*

MADE IN USA

INSTRUCTIONS

With Red, ch 119{155}.

Row 1 (Right side): Sc in 🎥 back ridge *(Fig. 1, page 46)* of second ch from hook and each ch across: 118{154} sc.

Note: Loop a short piece of yarn around any stitch to mark Row 1 as **right** side.

Row 2: Ch 3 (**counts as first dc, now and throughout**), turn; dc in next sc and in each sc across.

Row 3: Ch 3, turn; dc in next dc, skip next dc, 3 dc in next dc, (skip next 2 dc, 3 dc in next dc) across to last 3 dc, skip next dc, dc in last 2 dc.

Row 4: Ch 3, turn; dc in next dc, skip next dc, 5 dc in next dc, skip next 2 dc, hdc in next dc, ★ skip next 2 dc, 5 dc in next dc, skip next 2 dc, hdc in next dc; repeat from ★ across to last 3 dc, skip next dc, dc in last 2 dc.

Rows 5-8: Ch 3, turn; dc in next dc, 5 dc in next hdc, skip next 2 dc, hdc in next dc, ★ skip next 2 dc, 5 dc in next hdc, skip next 2 dc, hdc in next dc; repeat from ★ across to last 4 dc, skip next 2 dc, dc in last 2 dc.

Finish off.

Row 9: With **right** side facing, 🎥 join Blue with sc *(see Joining With Sc, page 46)* in first dc; sc in next dc and in each st across.

Row 10: Ch 3, turn; dc in next sc and in each sc across; finish off.

Row 11: With **right** side facing, 🎥 join Red with dc *(see Joining With Dc, page 46)* in first dc; dc in next dc, skip next dc, 3 dc in next dc, (skip next 2 dc, 3 dc in next dc) across to last 3 dc, skip next dc, dc in last 2 dc.

Repeat Rows 4-11 for pattern until piece measures approximately 46½{59}"/118{150} cm from beginning ch, ending by working Row 8; do **not** finish off.

Next Row: Ch 1, turn; sc in each st across.

Next Row: Ch 3, turn; dc in next sc and in each sc across.

Last Row: Ch 1, turn; sc in each dc across; finish off.

BADGE OF COURAGE

Shown on page 15.

 **EASY +**

SHOPPING LIST

Yarn (Medium Weight) **4** MEDIUM

[7 ounces, 370 yards

(198 grams, 338 meters) per skein]:

☐ 5{8} skeins

When purchasing yarn, reference the

Blue number for skeins needed for

the Lap Robe and the Pink number for

skeins needed for the Afghan.

Crochet Hook

☐ Size I (5.5 mm)

or size needed for gauge

SIZE INFORMATION

Finished Sizes

Lab Robe: 36½" x 50½" (92.5 cm x 128.5 cm)

Afghan: 48½" x 62½" (123 cm x 159 cm)

Size Note: We have printed the instructions for the sizes in different colors to make it easier for you to find:

• Lap Robe in Blue

• Afghan in Pink

Instructions in Black apply to both sizes.

GAUGE INFORMATION

In pattern, 12 sts = 4" (10 cm);

one repeat (Rows 7-18) = 6" (15.25 cm)

Gauge Swatch: 8¾"w x 5¾"h (22.25 cm x 14.5 cm)

Ch 27.

Work same as Instructions, page 14, for 12 rows: 26 sts.

Finish off.

Our photography model was made using

Red Heart® With Love®

MADE IN USA

STITCH GUIDE

📹 FRONT POST DOUBLE CROCHET
(abbreviated FPdc)

YO, insert hook from **front** to **back** around post of dc indicated *(Fig. 4, page 47)*, YO and pull up a loop (3 loops on hook), (YO and draw through 2 loops on hook) twice.

INSTRUCTIONS

Ch 111{147}.

Row 1: Sc in 📹 back ridge *(Fig. 1, page 46)* of second ch from hook and each ch across: 110{146} sc.

Row 2 (Right side)**:** Ch 1, turn; hdc in first sc and in each sc across.

Row 3: Ch 3 (**counts as first dc, now and throughout**), turn; dc in next hdc and in each hdc across.

Row 4: Ch 1, turn; sc in each dc across.

Row 5: Ch 1, turn; hdc in first sc and in each sc across.

Row 6: Ch 3, turn; dc in next hdc and in each hdc across.

Row 7: Ch 1, turn; hdc in first dc, dc in next 2 sts, work FPdc around next dc, (dc in next dc, work FPdc around next dc) 3 times, ★ dc in next 5 sts, work FPdc around next dc, (dc in next dc, work FPdc around next dc) 3 times; repeat from ★ across to last 4 sts, dc in last 4 sts.

Rows 8-12: Ch 1, turn; hdc in first dc, dc in next 2 dc, work FPdc around next dc, (dc in next FPdc, work FPdc around next dc) 3 times, ★ dc in next 5 sts, work FPdc around next dc, (dc in next FPdc, work FPdc around next dc) 3 times; repeat from ★ across to last 4 sts, dc in last 4 sts.

Row 13: Ch 1, turn; hdc in first dc, work FPdc around next dc, dc in next 9 sts, ★ work FPdc around next dc, dc in next dc, work FPdc around next dc, dc in next 9 sts; repeat from ★ across to last 3 sts, work FPdc around next dc, dc in last 2 sts.

Rows 14-18: Ch 1, turn; hdc in first dc, work FPdc around next dc, dc in next 9 sts, ★ work FPdc around next dc, dc in next FPdc, work FPdc around next dc, dc in next 9 sts; repeat from ★ across to last 3 sts, work FPdc around next dc, dc in last 2 sts.

Rows 19 thru 96{120}: Repeat Rows 7-18, 6{8} times; then repeat Rows 7-12 once **more**.

Row 97{121}: Ch 3, turn; dc in next dc and in each st across.

Row 98{122}: Ch 1, turn; hdc in first dc and in each dc across.

Row 99{123}: Ch 1, turn; sc in each hdc across.

Row 100{124}: Ch 3, turn; dc in next sc and in each sc across.

Row 101{125}: Ch 1, turn; hdc in first dc and in each dc across.

Row 102{126}: Ch 1, turn; sc in each hdc across; finish off.

Crocheted in rich purple, our Badge of Courage afghan is designed to honor recipients of the Purple Heart Medal, which is awarded to members of the Armed Forces who were wounded or killed in service. Established in 1782 by General George Washington, the award reflects his desire to honor "not only instances of unusual gallantry, but also of extraordinary fidelity and essential service in any way."

CAMOUFLAGE

 **EASY**

SHOPPING LIST

Yarn (Medium Weight)

[5 ounces, 244 yards
(141 grams, 223 meters) per skein]:

☐ 6{9} skeins

When purchasing yarn, reference
the Blue number for skeins needed
for the Lap Robe and the Pink
number for skeins needed for the
Afghan.

Crochet Hook

☐ Size I (5.5 mm)

or size needed for gauge

SIZE INFORMATION

Finished Sizes

Lab Robe: 36" x 48" (91.5 cm x 122 cm)

Afghan: 49" x 60" (124.5 cm x 152.5 cm)

Size Note: We have printed the instructions for the sizes in
different colors to make it easier for you to find:

• Lap Robe in Blue

• Afghan in Pink

Instructions in Black apply to both sizes.

GAUGE INFORMATION

In pattern, 2 repeats (14 sts) and 10 rows = 4¼" (10.75 cm)

Gauge Swatch: 4¼" (10.75 cm) square

Ch 15.

Work same as Instructions, page 24, for 10 rows: 14 sts.

Finish off.

Camouflage continued on page 24.

DESERT RIPPLES

 **EASY**

SHOPPING LIST

Yarn (Medium Weight)

[5 ounces, 244 yards
(141 grams, 223 meters) per skein]:

☐ 6{9} skeins

When purchasing yarn, reference the Blue number for skeins needed for the Lap Robe and the Pink number for skeins needed for the Afghan.

Crochet Hook

☐ Size I (5.5 mm)

or size needed for gauge

SIZE INFORMATION

Finished Sizes

Lab Robe: 36" x 48" (91.5 cm x 122 cm)

Afghan: 48" x 60" (122 cm x 152.5 cm)

Size Note: We have printed the instructions for the sizes in different colors to make it easier for you to find:

• Lap Robe in Blue

• Afghan in Pink

Instructions in Black apply to both sizes.

GAUGE INFORMATION

In pattern, 2 repeats (18 sts) (from point to point) = 4" (10 cm);
    8 rows = 3¼" (8.25 cm)

Gauge Swatch: 4"w x 3¼"h (10 cm x 8.25 cm)

Ch 17.

Work same as Instructions, page 25, for 8 rows: 18 sts.

Finish off.

Desert Ripples continued on page 25.

Our photography model was made using *Red Heart® Super Saver®*

MADE IN USA

DRESS BLUES

EASY

SIZE INFORMATION

Finished Sizes
Lab Robe: 36" x 49" (91.5 cm x 124.5 cm)
Afghan: 48" x 61" (122 cm x 155 cm)

Size Note: We have printed the instructions for the sizes in
different colors to make it easier for you to find:
• Lap Robe in Blue
• Afghan in Pink
Instructions in Black apply to both sizes.

GAUGE INFORMATION

In pattern, 14 sts = 4¼" (10.75 cm); 8 rows = 3" (7.5 cm)
Gauge Swatch: 4¼"w x 3¼"h (10.75 cm x 8.25 cm)
Ch 15.
Work same as Instructions, page 25, for 9 rows: 14 sts.
Finish off.

Dress Blues continued on page 25.

**Our photography
model was made using
*Red Heart® Super Saver®***

MADE IN USA

EARTH & SKY

SHOPPING LIST

Yarn (Medium Weight)

[5 ounces, 244 yards
(141 grams, 223 meters) per skein]:

☐ 6{9} skeins

When purchasing yarn, reference
the Blue number for skeins needed
for the Lap Robe and the Pink
number for skeins needed for the
Afghan.

Crochet Hook

☐ Size I (5.5 mm)

or size needed for gauge

Our photography
model was made using
Red Heart® Super Saver®

MADE IN USA

SIZE INFORMATION

Finished Sizes

Lab Robe: 36" x 48" (91.5 cm x 122 cm)

Afghan: 48" x 60" (122 cm x 152.5 cm)

Size Note: We have printed the instructions for the sizes in different
colors to make it easier for you to find:

• Lap Robe in Blue

• Afghan in Pink

Instructions in Black apply to both sizes.

GAUGE INFORMATION

In pattern, 15 sts = 5" (12.75 cm); 6 rows = 2¾" (7 cm)

Gauge Swatch: 5"w x 2¾"h (12.75 cm x 7 cm)

Ch 16.

Work same as Instructions, page 24, for 6 rows: 15 sts.

Finish off.

───── STITCH GUIDE ─────

🎥 **TREBLE CROCHET** *(abbreviated tr)*

YO twice, insert hook in st indicated, YO and pull up a loop (4 loops
on hook), (YO and draw through 2 loops on hook) 3 times.

EARTH & SKY

Continued from page 22.

INSTRUCTIONS

Ch 109{145}.

Row 1 (Right side): Sc in 📷 back ridge (*Fig. 1, page 46*) of second ch from hook and each ch across: 108{144} sc.

Rows 2 and 3: Ch 1, turn; sc in each sc across.

Rows 4-6: Ch 3 (**counts as first dc**), turn; skip next st, tr in next st, working **behind** tr just made, dc in skipped st, ★ dc in next st, skip next st, tr in next st, working **behind** tr just made, dc in skipped st; repeat from ★ across.

Rows 7-9: Ch 1, turn; sc in each st across.

Repeat Rows 4-9 for pattern until piece measures approximately 48{60}"/122{152.5} cm from beginning ch, ending by working Row 9.

Finish off.

CAMOUFLAGE

Continued from page 16.

INSTRUCTIONS

Ch 120{162}.

Row 1 (Right side): Sc in 📷 back ridge (*Fig. 1, page 46*) of second ch from hook and each ch across: 119{161} sc.

Row 2: Ch 1, turn; sc in first sc, hdc in next sc, skip next sc, 3 dc in next sc, skip next sc, hdc in next sc, ★ sc in next 2 sc, hdc in next sc, skip next sc, 3 dc in next s skip next sc, hdc in next sc; repeat from ★ across to last sc, sc in last sc.

Row 3: Ch 3 (**counts as first dc**), turn; hdc in next hdc, sk next dc, 3 sc in next dc, skip next dc, hdc in next hdc, ★ d in next 2 sc, hdc in next hdc, skip next dc, 3 sc in next dc, skip next dc, hdc in next hdc; repeat from ★ across to last sc, dc in last sc.

Row 4: Ch 1, turn; sc in first dc, hdc in next hdc, skip next sc, 3 dc in next sc, skip next sc, hdc in next hdc, ★ sc in next 2 dc, hdc in next hdc, skip next sc, 3 dc in next sc, skip next sc, hdc in next hdc; repeat from ★ across to last dc, sc in last dc.

Repeat Rows 3 and 4 for pattern until piece measures approximately 47¾{59¾}"/121.5{152} cm from beginning ch, ending by working Row 3.

Last Row: Ch 1, turn; sc in each st across; finish off.

DESERT RIPPLES

Continued from page 18.

INSTRUCTIONS

Ch 161{215}.

Row 1 (Right side):
Working in  back ridge *(Fig. 1, page 46)* of chs, sc in second ch from hook and in next 2 chs, 3 sc in next ch, sc in next 3 chs, ★ skip next 2 chs, sc in next 3 chs, 3 sc in next ch, sc in next 3 chs; repeat from ★ across: 162{216} sc.

Rows 2-4: Ch 1, turn; working in  Front Loops Only *(Fig. 2, page 46)*, skip first sc, sc in next 3 sc, 3 sc in next sc, sc in next 3 sc, ★ skip next 2 sc, sc in next 3 sc, 3 sc in next sc, sc in next 3 sc; repeat from ★ across, leave remaining sc unworked.

Rows 5-8: Ch 1, turn; working in Back Loops Only *(Fig. 2, page 46)*, skip first sc, sc in next 3 sc, 3 sc in next sc, sc in next 3 sc, ★ skip next 2 sc, sc in next 3 sc, 3 sc in next sc, sc in next 3 sc; repeat from ★ across, leave remaining sc unworked.

Rows 9-12: Ch 1, turn; working in Front Loops Only, skip first sc, sc in next 3 sc, 3 sc in next sc, sc in next 3 sc, ★ skip next 2 sc, sc in next 3 sc, 3 sc in next sc, sc in next 3 sc; repeat from ★ across, leave remaining sc unworked.

Repeat Rows 5-12 for pattern until piece measures approximately 48{60}"/122{152.5} cm from beginning ch, ending by working Row 7.

Finish off.

DRESS BLUES

Continued from page 20.

INSTRUCTIONS

Ch 119{159}.

Row 1 (Right side):
Sc in  back ridge *(Fig. 1, page 46)* of second ch from hook and each ch across: 118{158} sc.

Row 2: Ch 1, turn; sc in first sc, sc in  Front Loop Only *(Fig. 2, page 46)* of each sc across to last sc, sc in **both** loops of last sc.

Rows 3-5: Ch 1, turn; sc in **both** loops of first sc, sc in Front Loop Only of each sc across to last sc, sc in **both** loops of last sc.

Rows 6-9: Ch 1, turn; sc in **both** loops of first sc, ★ skip next st, sc in Front Loop Only of next st, dc in free loop *(Fig. 3a, page 46)* of same st; repeat from ★ across to last st, sc in **both** loops of last sc.

Rows 10-13: Ch 1, turn; sc in **both** loops of first sc, sc in Front Loop Only of each st across to last sc, sc in **both** loops of last sc.

Repeat Rows 6-13 for pattern until piece measures approximately 48{60}"/122{152.5} cm from beginning ch, ending by working Row 9.

Last 5 Rows: Ch 1, turn; sc in **both** loops of first sc, sc in Front Loop Only of each st across to last sc, sc in **both** loops of last sc.

Finish off.

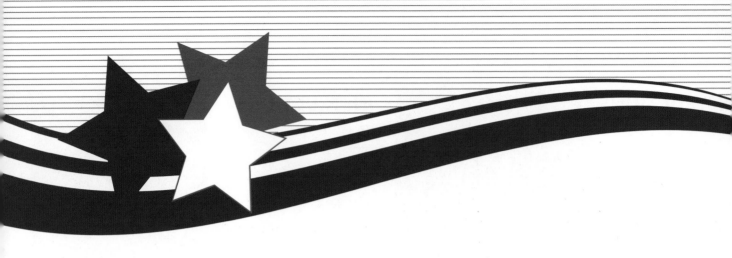

STARS & STRIPES

 EASY +

SIZE INFORMATION

Finished Sizes

Lab Robe: 37" x 49½" (94 cm x 125.5 cm)

Afghan: 47½" x 60½" (120.5 cm x 153.5 cm)

Size Note: We have printed the instructions for the sizes in different colors to make it easier for you to find:

• Lap Robe in Blue

• Afghan in Pink

Instructions in Black apply to both sizes.

GAUGE INFORMATION

14 hdc = 4" (10 cm); 14 rows = 5" (12.75 cm)

Gauge Swatch: 5½" (14 cm) square

Work same as Star Square, page 28: 72 sc.

Our photography model was made using *Red Heart® With Love®*

MADE IN USA

INSTRUCTIONS

Star Square [Make 36{55}]

With White, ch 3; join with slip st to form a ring.

Rnd 1 (Right side): Ch 1, 6 sc in ring; join with slip st to first sc.

Note: Loop a short piece of yarn around any stitch to mark Rnd 1 as **right** side.

Rnd 2: Ch 1, 2 sc in same st and in each sc around; join with slip st to  Front Loop Only *(Fig. 2, page 46)* of first sc: 12 sc.

Rnd 3 (Points): Ch 4, sc in second ch from hook, hdc in next ch, dc in next ch, ★ slip st in Front Loop Only of next 2 sc, ch 4, sc in second ch from hook, hdc in next ch, dc in next ch; repeat from ★ 4 times **more**, slip st in Front Loop Only of last sc, place marker around  free loop *(Fig. 3a, page 47)* of same sc for st placement: 6 points.

Rnd 4 (Trim): Skip first slip st, sc in  free loops of first 3 chs *(Fig. 3b, page 47)*, ch 3, sc in next sc and in next 2 sts, ★ skip next 2 slip sts, sc in free loops of next 3 chs, ch 3, sc in next sc and in next 2 sts; repeat from ★ 4 times **more**, skip last slip st and join with slip st to first sc, finish off:

Rnd 5: With **right** side facing and working behind last 2 rnds and in free loops of Rnd 2,  join Blue with dc *(see Joining With Dc, page 46)* in marked sc; dc in same st, 2 dc in each sc around; join with slip st to first dc: 24 dc.

Rnd 6: Ch 3 (**counts as first dc, now and throughout**), dc in same st, ch 2, skip next dc, ★ 2 dc in next dc, ch 2, skip next dc; repeat from ★ around; join with slip st to first dc: 24 dc and 12 ch-2 sps.

Rnd 7: Slip st in next dc and in next ch-2 sp, ch 1, (sc, hdc) in same sp, working in center ch of ch-3 on next point, dc in same ch-2 sp as last hdc made, (hdc, sc) in same sp on Rnd 6 as last dc made, (sc, hdc, dc, hdc, sc) in next ch-2 sp, ★ (sc, hdc) in next ch-2 sp, working in center ch of ch-3 on next point, dc in same ch-2 sp as last hdc made, (hdc, sc) in same sp on Rnd 6 as last dc made, (sc, hdc, dc, hdc, sc) in next ch-2 sp; repeat from ★ around; join with slip st to first sc: 60 sts.

Rnd 8: Slip st in next 2 sts, ch 3, (2 dc, ch 2, 3 dc) in same st, ch 3, skip next 4 sts, (sc in next dc, ch 3, skip next 4 sts) twice, ★ (3 dc, ch 2, 3 dc) in next dc, ch 3, skip next 4 sts, (sc in next dc, ch 3, skip next 4 sts) twice; repeat from ★ 2 times **more**; join with slip st to first dc: 32 sts and 16 sps.

Rnd 9: Ch 1, sc in same st and in next 2 dc, 3 sc in next corner ch-2 sp, sc in next 3 dc, 3 sc in each of next 3 ch-3 sps, ★ sc in next 3 dc, 3 sc in next corner ch-2 sp, sc in next 3 dc, 3 sc in each of next 3 ch-3 sps; repeat from ★ 2 times **more**; join with slip st to first sc, finish off: 72 sc.

Assembly

With **wrong** sides together, working through **both** loops on **both** pieces, and using Blue,  whipstitch *(Fig. 6, page 47)* Star Squares together forming 4{5} vertical Strips of 9{11} Squares each, beginning in center sc of first 3-sc group and ending in center sc of next 3-sc group. Do **not** join Strips.

Stripes

Row 1: With **right** side of one strip facing and working across long edge, join Red with slip st in center sc of first corner; ch 1, hdc in same st, hdc in next 17 sc, hdc in same sc as joining on same Square and in same st as joining on next Square; repeat from ★ 7{9} times **more**, hdc in next 8 sc, leave remaining sts unworked, place marker around last hdc made to mark bottom edge: 171{209} hdc.

Row 2: Ch 1, turn; hdc in first hdc and each hdc across; finish off.

Row 3: With **right** side facing, join White with slip st in first hdc; ch 1, hdc in same st and in each hdc across.

Row 4: Ch 1, turn; hdc in first hdc and each hdc across; finish off.

Row 5: With **right** side facing, join Red with slip st in first hdc; ch 1, hdc in same st and in each hdc across.

Row 6: Ch 1, turn; hdc in first hdc and each hdc across; finish off.

Rows 7-14: Repeat Rows 3-6 twice.

Work Stripes on 3{4} strips, leaving one strip without Stripes to use for outside edge.

ASSEMBLY

Using Placement Diagram as a guide: Place **wrong** sides of two Strips together, matching Star Square edge of one Strip to Stripes edge on next Strip. With Red and working in **both** loops on **both** pieces, whipstitch Strips together. Whipstitch remaining Strips together in same manner.

LAP ROBE
PLACEMENT DIAGRAM

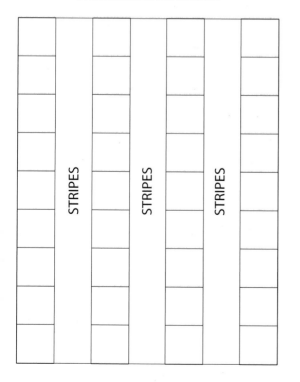

AFGHAN
PLACEMENT DIAGRAM

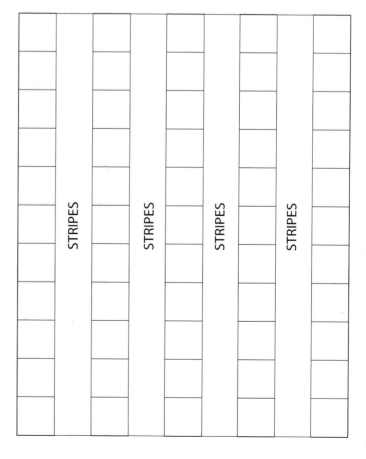

INDEPENDENCE DAY

EASY +

SHOPPING LIST

Yarn (Medium Weight)

[7 ounces, 370 yards
(198 grams, 338 meters) per skein]:

☐ Ecru - 4 skeins

☐ Red - 3 skeins

☐ Blue - 2 skeins

Crochet Hook

☐ Size J (6 mm)

or size needed for gauge

Additional Supplies

☐ Yarn needle

Finished Size: 45" x 70" (114.5 cm x 178 cm)

GAUGE INFORMATION

In pattern, (3 dc, ch 1) 4 times = 4¼ " (10.75 cm); 7 rows = 4" (10 cm)

Gauge Swatch: 4" (10 cm) (straight edge to straight edge) and
4½" (11.5 cm) (point to point)
Work same as Motif, page 32: 36 dc and 6 ch-2 sps.

STITCH GUIDE

TREBLE CROCHET *(abbreviated tr)*

YO twice, insert hook in st or sp indicated, YO and pull up a loop (4 loops on hook), (YO and draw through 2 loops on hook) 3 times.

RIGHT DECREASE (uses next 2 dc)

YO twice, insert hook in next dc, YO and pull up a loop, (YO and draw through 2 loops on hook) twice, YO, insert hook in next dc, YO and pull up a loop, YO and draw through 2 loops on hook, YO and draw through all 3 loops on hook.

LEFT DECREASE (uses next 2 dc)

YO, insert hook in next dc, YO and pull up a loop, YO and draw through 2 loops on hook, YO twice, insert hook in next dc, YO and pull up a loop, (YO and draw through 2 loops on hook) twice, YO and draw through all 3 loops on hook.

CLUSTER (uses next 2 sps and next joining)

YO 3 times, insert hook in next sp, YO and pull up a loop, (YO and draw through 2 loops on hook) 3 times, YO 3 times, insert hook in joining, YO and pull up a loop, (YO and draw through 2 loops on hook) 3 times, YO 3 times, insert hook in next sp, YO and pull up a loop, (YO and draw through 2 loops on hook) 3 times, YO and draw through all 4 loops on hook.

INSTRUCTIONS
Star Field
MOTIF (Make 46)

With Ecru, ch 3; join with slip st to form a ring.

Rnd 1 (Right side): Ch 1, 12 sc in ring; join with slip st to first sc.

Note: Loop a short piece of yarn around any stitch to mark Rnd 1 as **right** side.

Rnd 2: 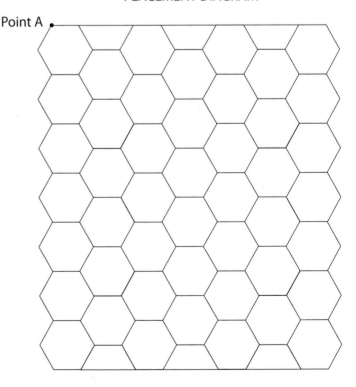 Ch 2, (YO, insert hook in **next** sc, YO and pull up a loop, YO and draw through 2 loops on hook) twice, YO and draw through all 3 loops on hook, ★ ch 4, YO, insert hook in **same** sc, YO and pull up a loop, YO and draw through 2 loops on hook, (YO, insert hook in **next** sc, YO and pull up a loop, YO and draw through 2 loops on hook) twice, YO and draw through all 4 loops on hook; repeat from ★ 4 times **more** working last st in same sc as beginning ch-2, ch 4; join with slip st to first st, finish off: 6 ch-4 sps.

Rnd 3: With **right** side facing, join Blue with slip st in any ch-4 sp; ch 1, 6 sc in same sp and in each ch-4 sp around; join with slip st to first sc: 36 sc.

Rnd 4: Ch 3 (**counts as first dc, now and throughout**), dc in next 2 sc, ch 2, (dc in next 6 sc, ch 2) 5 times, dc in last 3 sc; join with slip st to first dc, finish off: 36 dc and 6 ch-2 sps.

HALF MOTIF (Make 6)

Row 1 (Right side): With Blue, ch 4, 8 dc in fourth ch from hook (**3 skipped chs count as first dc**): 9 dc.

Note: Mark Row 1 as **right** side.

Row 2: Ch 1, turn; sc in first dc, (2 sc in next dc, sc in next dc) across: 13 sc.

Row 3: Ch 3, turn; dc in same st and in next sc, 2 dc in next sc, dc in next sc, ★ (dc, ch 2, dc) in next sc, dc in next sc, 2 dc in next sc, dc in next sc; repeat from ★ once **more**, (dc, ch 3, slip st) in last sc; finish off: 20 sts and 2 ch-2 sps.

ASSEMBLY

With **wrong** sides together and Blue working through **both** loops, and using Placement Diagram as a guide 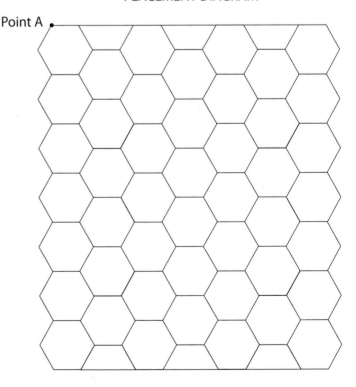 whipstitch (*Fig. 6, page 47*) Motif and Half Motifs together forming 4 vertical strips of 7 Motifs **and** 3 vertical strips of 6 Motifs and 2 Half Motifs, beginning in second ch of first corner ch-2 and ending in first ch of next corner ch-2; then whipstitch strips together in same manner.

PLACEMENT DIAGRAM

Point A

DGING

'ith **right** side facing, join Blue with
p st in ch-2 sp at point A; † ch 4,
 in next dc, work right decrease,
c in next dc, hdc in next 2 dc, sc in
ext ch-2 sp, hdc in next 2 dc, dc in
ext dc, work left decrease, ★ tr in
ext dc, work Cluster, tr in next dc,
ork right decrease, dc in next dc,
dc in next 2 dc, sc in next ch-2 sp,
dc in next 2 dc, dc in next dc, work
ft decrease; repeat from ★ 5 times
ore, tr in next dc and in next
h-2 sp, 3 sc around post of tr just
ade, sc in same sp as tr, sc in next
 dc and in next sp; ♥ working in end
f rows of Half Motif, 2 sc in first row,
 in next row, 2 sc in next row, sc in
free loop of ch (*Fig. 3b, page 47*)
 base of 9-dc group, 2 sc in next
w, sc in next row, 2 sc in next row,
 in next sp on next Motif, sc in
ext 6 dc and in next sp ♥; repeat
om ♥ to ♥ 2 times **more** †, slip st in
ame sp as last sc made, repeat from
 to † once, 3 sc around beginning
h-4; join with slip st to top of
eginning ch-4, finish off.

STRIPES

With Red, ch 265.

Row 1 (Right side)**:** Dc in fourth ch
from hook and in next ch (**3 skipped
chs count as first dc**), ★ ch 1, skip
next ch, dc in next 3 chs; repeat from
★ across: 66 3-dc groups.

Note: Mark Row 1 as **right** side.

Row 2: Ch 5 (**counts as first dc plus
ch 2, now and throughout**), turn;
3 dc in next ch-1 sp, (ch 1, 3 dc in
next ch-1 sp) across to last 3 dc,
ch-2, skip next 2 dc, dc in last dc:
65 3-dc groups.

Row 3: Ch 3, turn; 2 dc in next
ch-2 sp, (ch 1, 3 dc in next ch-1 sp)
across to last ch-2 sp, ch 1, 2 dc in last
sp, dc in last dc: 66 3-dc groups.

Row 4: Ch 5, turn; 3 dc in next
ch-1 sp, (ch 1, 3 dc in next ch-1 sp)
across to last 3 dc, ch 2, skip next
2 dc, dc in last dc: 65 3-dc groups.

Rows 5 and 6: Repeat Rows 3 and 4,
changing to Ecru (*Fig. 5, page 47*)
at end of Row 6.

Rows 7-12: Repeat Rows 3 and 4,
3 times, changing to Red at end of
Row 12.

Rows 13-18: Repeat Rows 3 and 4,
3 times, changing to Ecru at end of
Row 18.

Rows 19-36: Repeat Rows 7-18 once,
then repeat Rows 7-12 once **more**.

Row 37: Ch 3, turn; 2 dc in next
ch-2 sp, (ch 1, 3 dc in next ch-1 sp) 39
times, leave remaining sts unworked:
40 3-dc groups.

Rows 38-42: Repeat Rows 2-6:
39 3-dc groups.

Rows 43-78: Repeat Rows 7-18,
3 times; at end of Row 78, do **not**
change colors and do **not** finish off.

EDGING

Ch 1, turn; using corresponding
color, sc evenly around entire piece
working 3 sc in each corner and
decreasing at inner corner; join with
slip st to first sc, finish off.

Whipstitch Star Field into upper
lefthand corner of Stripes.

Design by Linda A. Daley.

GRATITUDE

 **EASY +**

SHOPPING LIST

Yarn (Medium Weight)

[7 ounces, 370 yards
(198 grams, 338 meters) per skein]:

☐ Grey - 2{3} skeins

☐ White - 2 skeins

☐ Black - 1{2} skein(s)

When purchasing yarn, reference the Blue number for skeins needed for the Lap Robe and the Pink number for skeins needed for the Afghan.

Crochet Hook

☐ Size I (5.5 mm)
    or size needed for gauge

Additional Supplies

☐ Yarn needle

Our photography model was made using *Red Heart® With Love®*

MADE IN USA

SIZE INFORMATION

Finished Sizes

Lab Robe: 37" x 48½" (94 cm x 123 cm)

Afghan: 49" x 64½" (124.5 cm x 164 cm)

Size Note: We have printed the instructions for the sizes in different colors to make it easier for you to find:

• Lap Robe in Blue

• Afghan in Pink

Instructions in Black apply to both sizes.

GAUGE INFORMATION

Each Strip = 6" (15.25 cm) wide

Gauge Swatch: 2½"w x 13½"h (6.25 cm x 34.25 cm)

With White, ch 36.

Rnds 1 and 2: Work same as Strip, page 36: 46 sc and 34 ch-2 sps.

Rnd 3: With **right** side facing, join Grey with slip st in first ch-2 sp; ch 3 (**counts as first dc**), dc in same sp, † (ch 1, dc in next ch-2 sp, ch 1, 2 dc in next ch-2 sp) 8 times, skip next sc, (ch 1, 2 dc in next sc) twice, ch 2, skip next sc, (2 dc in next sc, ch 1) twice, skip next sc †, 2 dc in next ch-2 sp, repeat from † to † once; join with slip st to first dc, finish off: 68 dc and 42 sps.

INSTRUCTIONS

Strip [Make 6{8}]

With White, ch 128{180}.

Rnd 1 (Right side)**:** Sc in second ch from hook, (ch 1, skip next ch, sc in next ch) across, ch 3; working in ▣ free loops of beginning ch *(Fig. 3b, page 47)*, sc in first ch, (ch 1, skip next ch, sc in next ch) across, ch 3; join with slip st to first sc, finish off: 128{180} sc and 128{180} sps.

Note: Loop a short piece of yarn around any stitch to mark Rnd 1 as **right** side.

Rnd 2: With **right** side facing, ▣ join Black with sc *(see Joining With Sc, page 46)* in same st as joining; (ch 2, sc in next sc) across to next ch-3 sp, 5 sc in ch-3 sp, sc in next sc, (ch 2, sc in next sc) across to last ch-3 sp, 5 sc in last ch-3 sp; join with slip st to first sc, finish off: 138{190} sc and 126{178} ch-2 sps.

Rnd 3: With **right** side facing, join Grey with slip st in first ch-2 sp; ch 3 **(counts as first dc, now and throughout)**, dc in same sp, † (ch 1, dc in next ch-2 sp, ch 1, 2 dc in next ch-2 sp) 31{44} times, skip next sc, (ch 1, 2 dc in next sc) twice, ch 2, skip next sc, (2 dc in next sc, ch 1) twice, skip next sc †, 2 dc in next ch-2 sp, repeat from † to † once; join with slip st to first dc, finish off: 206{284} dc and 134{186} sps.

Rnd 4: With **right** side facing, join Black with slip st in ch-2 sp on either end; ch 3, (2 dc, ch 2, 3 dc) in same sp, (ch 1, 3 dc in next ch-1 sp) 3 times, (ch 1, skip next ch-1 sp, 3 dc in next ch-1 sp) across to ch-1 sp before next ch-2 sp, ch 1, 3 dc in next ch-1 sp, ch 1, (3 dc, ch 2, 3 dc) in next ch-2 sp, (ch 1, 3 dc in next ch-1 sp) 3 times, (ch 1, skip next ch-1 sp, 3 dc in next ch-1 sp) across to last ch-1 sp, ch 1, 3 dc in last ch-1 sp, ch 1; join with slip st to first dc, finish off: 74{100} dc and 74{100} sps.

Rnd 5: With **right** side facing, join Grey with slip st in first ch-2 sp; ch 3, 4 dc in same sp and in each ch-1 sp across to next ch-2 sp, 5 dc in next ch-2 sp, 4 dc in next ch-1 sp and in each ch-1 sp across; join with slip st to first dc, finish off: 298{402} dc.

Rnd 6: With **right** side facing, join White with slip st in same st as joining; ch 3, dc in same st, 2 dc in each of next 8 dc, dc in next dc, place marker around dc just made for Assembly, dc in next dc and in each dc across to 4-dc group before next 5-dc group, place marker around last dc made for Assembly, 2 dc in each of next 13 dc, dc in next dc, place marker around dc just made for Assembly, dc in next dc and in each dc across to last 4 dc, place marker around last dc made for Assembly, 2 dc in each of last 4 dc; join with slip st first dc, finish off: 324{428} dc.

Assembly

With **wrong** sides of two Strips together and working through **both** loops on **both** pieces, using White, ▣ whipstitch *(Fig. 6, page 47)* Strips together, beginning in first marked dc and ending in next marked dc.

Whipstitch remaining Strips together in same manner.

PINK CAMO

Shown on page 39.

 ■■□□ **EASY**

SHOPPING LIST

Yarn (Medium Weight)

[5 ounces, 244 yards
(141 grams, 223 meters) per skein]:

☐ 6{10} skeins

When purchasing yarn, reference
the Blue number for skeins needed
for the Lap Robe and the Pink
number for skeins needed for the
Afghan.

Crochet Hook

☐ Size I (5.5 mm)

   or size needed for gauge

SIZE INFORMATION

Finshed Sizes
Lab Robe: 35½" x 48½" (90 cm x 123 cm)
Afghan: 48" x 60" (122 cm x 152.5 cm)

Size Note: We have printed the instructions for the sizes in different
colors to make it easier for you to find:

• Lap Robe in Blue

• Afghan in Pink

Instructions in Black apply to both sizes.

GAUGE INFORMATION

In pattern, 13 sc = 4½" (11.5 cm);
    Rows 2-9 = 3¼" (8.25 cm)
Gauge Swatch: 4½"w x 3½"h (11.5 cm x 9 cm)
Ch 14.
Work same as Instructions, page 38, for 9 rows: 13 sc.
Finish off.

★ ★ ★
**Our photography
model was made using
*Red Heart® Super Saver®***

MADE IN USA

STITCH GUIDE

BEGINNING CLUSTER
(uses one sc)

★ YO, insert hook in sc indicated, YO and pull up a loop, YO and draw through 2 loops on hook; repeat from ★ once **more**, YO and draw through all 3 loops on hook.

CLUSTER (uses one sc)

★ YO, insert hook in sc indicated, YO and pull up a loop, YO and draw through 2 loops on hook; repeat from ★ 3 times **more**, YO and draw through all 5 loops on hook.

ENDING CLUSTER (uses one sc)

★ YO, insert hook in sc indicated, YO and pull up a loop, YO and draw through 2 loops on hook; repeat from ★ 2 times **more**, YO and draw through all 4 loops on hook.

INSTRUCTIONS

Ch 104{140}.

Row 1 (Right side): Sc in back ridge (*Fig. 1, page 46*) of second ch from hook and in each ch across: 103{139} sc.

Row 2: Ch 2, turn; work beginning Cluster in first sc, dc in next 5 sc, (work Cluster in next sc, dc in next 5 sc) across to last sc, work ending Cluster in last sc: 85{115} dc and 18{24} Clusters.

Row 3: Ch 1, turn; sc in each st across: 103{139} sc.

Row 4: Ch 2, turn; work beginning Cluster in first sc, dc in next 2 sc, work Cluster in next sc, (dc in next 5 sc, work Cluster in next sc) across to last 3 sc, dc in next 2 sc, work ending Cluster in last sc: 84{114} dc and 19{25} Clusters.

Row 5: Ch 1, turn; sc in each st across: 103{139} sc.

Row 6: Ch 2, turn; work beginning Cluster in first sc, dc in next 5 sc, (work Cluster in next sc, dc in next 5 sc) across to last sc, work ending Cluster in last sc: 85{115} dc and 18{24} Clusters.

Rows 7-9: Ch 1, turn; sc in each st across: 103{139} sc.

Row 10: Ch 2, turn; work beginning Cluster in first sc, dc in next 2 sc, work Cluster in next sc, (dc in next 5 sc, work Cluster in next sc) across to last 3 sc, dc in next 2 sc, work ending Cluster in last sc: 84{114} dc and 19{25} Clusters.

Row 11: Ch 1, turn; sc in each st across: 103{139} sc.

Row 12: Ch 2, turn; work beginning Cluster in first sc, dc in next 5 sc, (work Cluster in next sc, dc in next 5 sc) across to last sc, work ending Cluster in last sc: 85{115} dc and 18{24} Clusters.

Row 13: Ch 1, turn; sc in each st across: 103{139} sc.

Row 14: Ch 2, turn; work beginning Cluster in first sc, dc in next 2 sc, wor Cluster in next sc, (dc in next 5 sc, work Cluster in next sc) across to last 3 sc, dc in next 2 sc, work ending Cluster in last sc: 84{114} dc and 19{25} Clusters.

Rows 15-17: Ch 1, turn; sc in each st across: 103{139} sc.

Repeat Rows 2-17 for pattern until piece measures approximately 48½{60}"/123{152.5} cm from beginning ch, ending by working Row 7.

Finish off.

PLATOON

 **EASY**

SIZE INFORMATION

Finished Sizes

Lab Robe: 36" x 47½" (91.5 cm x 120.5 cm)

Afghan: 48" x 62½" (122 cm x 159 cm)

Size Note: We have printed the instructions for the sizes in different colors to make it easier for you to find:

• Lap Robe in Blue

• Afghan in Pink

Instructions in Black apply to both sizes.

GAUGE INFORMATION

In pattern, 15 sts = 4¼" (10.75 cm);

  Rows 1-8 = 2¼" (5.75 cm)

  Rows 9-28 =7½" (19 cm)

Gauge Swatch: 4¼"w x 3¼"h (10.75 cm x 8.25 cm)

Ch 16.

Work same as Instructions, page 44, for 10 rows: 15 sc.

Finish off.

Platoon continued on page 44.

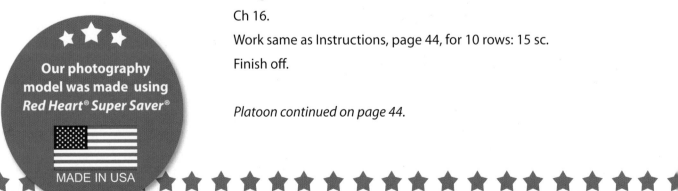

Our photography model was made using *Red Heart® Super Saver®*

MADE IN USA

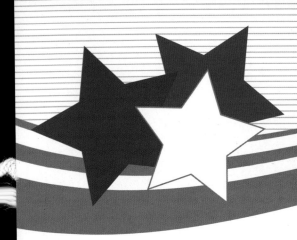

URBAN CAMO

■■□□ **EASY**

SHOPPING LIST

Yarn (Medium Weight)

[5 ounces, 244 yards
(141 grams, 223 meters) per skein]:

☐ 7{11} skeins

When purchasing yarn, reference the Blue number for skeins needed for the Lap Robe and the Pink number for skeins needed for the Afghan.

Crochet Hook

☐ Size I (5.5 mm)

or size needed for gauge

SIZE INFORMATION

Finished Sizes

Lab Robe: 36" x 48" (91.5 cm x 122 cm)

Afghan: 48" x 60" (122 cm x 152.5 cm)

Size Note: We have printed the instructions for the sizes in different colors to make it easier for you to find:

• Lap Robe in Blue

• Afghan in Pink

Instructions in Black apply to both sizes.

GAUGE INFORMATION

In pattern, 14 sts = 4" (10 cm);

2 repeats (Rows 1-6) = 2¼" (5.75 cm)

Gauge Swatch: 4"w x 2¼"h (10 cm x 5.75 cm)

Ch 15.

Work same as Instructions, page 44, for 6 rows: 14 sts.

Finish off.

Urban Camo continued on page 44.

Our photography model was made using *Red Heart® Super Saver®*

MADE IN USA

URBAN CAMO

Continued from page 42.

INSTRUCTIONS

Ch 127{169}.

Row 1 (Right side)**:** Hdc in 📹 back ridge *(Fig. 1, page 46)* of second ch from hook and each ch across: 126{168} hdc.

Note: Loop a short piece of yarn around any stitch to mark Row 1 as **right** side.

Row 2: Ch 1, turn; sc in Back Loop Only of each hdc across *(Fig. 2, page 46)*.

Rows 3 and 4: Ch 1, turn; hdc in Back Loop Only of first st and each st across.

Row 5: Ch 1, turn; sc in Back Loop Only of each st across.

Repeat Rows 3-5 for pattern until piece measures approximately 48{60}"/122{152.5} cm from beginning ch, ending by working a **right** side hdc row.

Finish off.

PLATOON

Continued from page 40.

INSTRUCTIONS

Ch 128{170}.

Row 1 (Right side)**:** Sc in 📹 back ridge of second ch from hook *(Fig. 1, page 46)* and each ch across: 127{169} sc.

Row 2: Ch 1, turn; sc in first sc, sc in 📹 Front Loop Only *(Fig. 2, page 46)* of next sc, ★ sc in 📹 Back Loop Only *(Fig. 2, page 46)* of next sc, sc in Front Loop Only of next sc; repeat from ★ across to last sc, sc in **both** loops of last sc.

Row 3: Ch 1, turn; sc in **both** loops of first sc, sc in Back Loop Only of next sc, ★ sc in Front Loop Only of next sc, sc in Back Loop Only of next sc; repeat from ★ across to last sc, sc in **both** loops of last sc.

Row 4: Ch 1, turn; sc in **both** loops of first sc, sc in Front Loop Only of next sc, ★ sc in Back Loop Only of next sc, sc in Front Loop Only of next sc; repeat from ★ across to last sc, sc in **both** loops of last sc.

Rows 5-8: Repeat Rows 3 and 4 twice.

Rows 9 and 10: Ch 1, turn; sc in **both** loops of first sc, sc in Front Loop Only of next sc and each sc across to last sc, sc in **both** loops of last sc.

Row 11: Ch 1, turn; hdc in **both** loops of first st, hdc in Front Loop Only of next st, ★ hdc in Back Loop Only of next st, hdc in Front Loop Only of next st; repeat from ★ across to last st, hdc in **both** loops of last st.

Row 12: Ch 1, turn; hdc in **both** loops of first hdc, hdc in Back Loop Only of next hdc, ★ hdc in Front Loop Only of next hdc, hdc in Back Loop Only of next hdc; repeat from ★ across to last hdc, hdc in **both** loops of last hdc.

Rows 13-18: Repeat Rows 11 and 12, 3 times.

Rows 19 and 20: Ch 1, turn; sc in **both** loops of first st, sc in Front Loop Only of next st and each st across to last st, sc in **both** loops of last st.

Rows 21-28: Repeat Rows 2 and 3, 4 times.

Repeat Rows 9-28 for pattern until piece measures approximately 47¾{60}"/121.5{152.5} cm from beginning ch, ending by working Row 28.

Last Row: Ch 1, turn; sc in both loops of each sc across; finish off.

GENERAL INSTRUCTIONS

ABBREVIATIONS

ch(s)	chain(s)
cm	centimeters
dc	double crochet(s)
FPdc	Front Post double crochet(s)
hdc	half double crochet(s)
mm	millimeters
Rnd(s)	Round(s)
sc	single crochet(s)
sp(s)	space(s)
st(s)	stitch(es)
tr	treble crochet(s)
YO	yarn over

SYMBOLS & TERMS

★ — work instructions following ★ as many **more** times as indicated in addition to the first time.

† to † or ♥ to ♥ — work all instructions from first † to second † or from first ♥ to second ♥ **as many** times as specified.

( ) or [ ] — work enclosed instructions **as many** times as specified by the number immediately following **or** work all enclosed instructions in the stitch or space indicated **or** contains explanatory remarks.

colon (:) — the number(s) given after a colon at the end of a row or round denote(s) the number of stitches or spaces you should have on that row or round.

CROCHET TERMINOLOGY	
UNITED STATES	INTERNATIONAL
slip stitch (slip st) =	single crochet (sc)
single crochet (sc) =	double crochet (dc)
half double crochet (hdc) =	half treble crochet (htr)
double crochet (dc) =	treble crochet(tr)
treble crochet (tr) =	double treble crochet (dtr)
double treble crochet (dtr) =	triple treble crochet (ttr)
triple treble crochet (tr tr) =	quadruple treble crochet (qtr)
skip =	miss

CROCHET HOOKS																	
U.S.	B-1	C-2	D-3	E-4	F-5	G-6	7	H-8	I-9	J-10	K-10½	L-11	M/N-13	N/P-15	P/Q	Q	S
Metric - mm	2.25	2.75	3.25	3.5	3.75	4	4.5	5	5.5	6	6.5	8	9	10	15	16	19

◼◻◻◻ **BEGINNER**	Projects for first-time crocheters using basic stitches. Minimal shaping.
◼◼◻◻ **EASY**	Projects using yarn with basic stitches, repetitive stitch patterns, simple color changes, and simple shaping and finishing.
◼◼◼◻ **INTERMEDIATE**	Projects using a variety of techniques, such as basic lace patterns or color patterns, mid-level shaping and finishing.
◼◼◼◼ **EXPERIENCED**	Projects with intricate stitch patterns, techniques and dimension, such as non-repeating patterns, multi-color techniques, fine threads, small hooks, detailed shaping and refined finishing.

GAUGE

Exact gauge is essential for proper size. Before beginning your project, make the sample swatch given in the individual instructions in the yarn and hook specified. After completing the swatch, measure it, counting your stitches and rows or rounds carefully. If your swatch is larger or smaller than specified, **make another, changing hook size to get the correct gauge**. Keep trying until you find the size hook that will give you the specified gauge.

JOINING WITH SC

When instructed to join with sc, begin with a slip knot on the hook. Insert the hook in the stitch or space indicated, YO and pull up a loop, YO and draw through both loops on the hook.

JOINING WITH DC

When instructed to join with dc, begin with a slip knot on the hook. YO, holding loop on the hook, insert the hook in the stitch or space indicated, YO and pull up a loop (3 loops on hook), (YO and draw through all 2 loops on hook) twice.

BACK RIDGE

Work only in loops indicated by arrows (*Fig. 1*).

Fig. 1

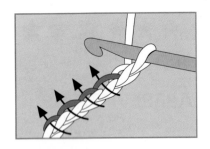

BACK OR FRONT LOOP ONLY

Work only in loop(s) indicated by arrow (*Fig. 2*).

Fig. 2

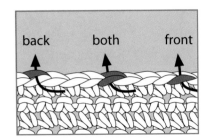

Yarn Weight Symbol & Names	LACE 0	SUPER FINE 1	FINE 2	LIGHT 3	MEDIUM 4	BULKY 5	SUPER BULKY 6
Type of Yarns in Category	Fingering, 10-count crochet thread	Sock, Fingering Baby	Sport, Baby	DK, Light Worsted	Worsted, Afghan, Aran	Chunky, Craft, Rug	Bulky, Roving
Crochet Gauge* Ranges in Single Crochet to 4" (10 cm)	32-42 double crochets**	21-32 sts	16-20 sts	12-17 sts	11-14 sts	8-11 sts	5-9 sts
Advised Hook Size Range	Steel*** 6,7,8 Regular hook B-1	B-1 to E-4	E-4 to 7	7 to I-9	I-9 to K-10.5	K-10.5 to M-13	M-13 and larger

*GUIDELINES ONLY: The chart above reflects the most commonly used gauges and hook sizes for specific yarn categories.

** Lace weight yarns are usually crocheted on larger-size hooks to create lacy openwork patterns. Accordingly, a gauge range is difficult to determine. Always follow the gauge stated in your pattern.

*** Steel crochet hooks are sized differently from regular hooks—the higher the number the smaller the hook, which is the reverse of regular hook sizing.

FREE LOOPS

After working in Back or Front Loops Only on a row or round, there will be a ridge of unused loops. These are called the free loops. Later, when instructed to work in free loops of the same row or round, work in these loops *(Fig. 3a)*.

When instructed to work in free loops of a chain, work in loop indicated by arrow *(Fig. 3b)*.

Fig. 3a

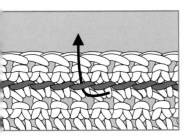

Fig. 3b

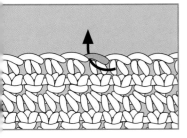

POST STITCH

Work around the post of stitch indicated, inserting the hook in direction of arrow *(Fig. 4)*.

Fig. 4

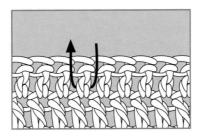

CHANGING COLORS

Work the last stitch to within one step of completion, hook new yarn *(Fig. 5)* and draw through all loops on hook. Cut old yarn and work over both ends unless otherwise instructed.

Fig. 5

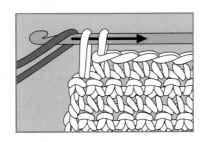

WHIPSTITCH

Place two Strips or Squares, with **wrong** sides together. Sew through both pieces once to secure the beginning of the seam, leaving an ample yarn end to weave in later. Insert the needle from **front** to **back** through **both** loops on **both** pieces *(Fig. 6)*. Bring the needle around and insert it from **front** to **back** through the next loops of both pieces. Continue in this manner across to corner, keeping the sewing yarn fairly loose.

Fig. 6

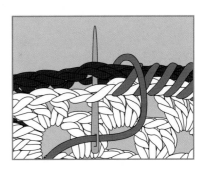

★★★★★★ YARN INFORMATION ★★★★★★

The projects in this book were made using Medium Weight yarn. Any brand of Medium Weight yarn may be used. It is best to refer to the yardage/meters when determining how many balls or skeins to purchase. Remember, to arrive at the finished size, it is the GAUGE/TENSION that is important, not the brand of yarn.

For your convenience, listed below are the specific yarns used to create our photography models.

AMERICAN HERO
Red Heart® Super Saver®
Red - #0332 Ranch Red
Tan - #0334 Buff
Blue - #0380 Windsor Blue

AMERICAN INSPIRATION
Red Heart® With Love®
Red - #1914 Berry Red
Blue - #1801 Navy

BADGE OF COURAGE
Red Heart® With Love®
#1542 Aubergine

CAMOUFLAGE
Red Heart® Super Saver®
#0971 Camouflage

DESERT RIPPLES
Red Heart® Super Saver®
#0991 Desert Camo

DRESS BLUES
Red Heart® Super Saver®
#0970 Dress Blues

EARTH & SKY
Red Heart® Super Saver®
#0928 Earth & Sky

STARS & STRIPES
Red Heart® With Love®
Blue - #1814 True Blue
White - #1001 White
Red - #1909 Holly Berry

INDEPENDENCE DAY
Red Heart® With Love®
Ecru - #1303 Aran
Red - #1915 Merlot
Blue - #1801 Navy

GRATITUDE
Red Heart® With Love®
Grey - #1401 Pewter
White - #1001 White
Black - #1012 Black

PINK CAMO
Red Heart® Super Saver®
#0972 Pink Camo

PLATOON
Red Heart® Super Saver®
#0988 Platoon

URBAN CAMO
Red Heart® Super Saver®
#0985 Urban Camo